# ONE NATION UNDER GOD

## America's Christian Heritage

Compiled and written by the staff
of the Christian Defense Fund

Published by the Christian Defense Fund

Copyright 1997 by the Christian Defense Fund. Printed in the United States by the Christian Defense Fund. All rights reserved.

Front cover illustration from Wood River Gallery, Mill Valley, CA

Suggested retail price for ONE NATION UNDER GOD is $6.95. Books are available for bulk purchases by writing to the Christian Defense Fund, 6564 Loisdale Court, Suite 320, Springfield, Virginia 22150

# WHY WE PUBLISHED THIS BOOK

American school children and college students today are being subjected to what we call "The Liberal History Lesson," which goes something like this. America, say liberals, was a product of the Enlightenment, which was a rejection of Christianity. America, say liberals, was founded primarily by Deists, not by Christians. The Constitution, say liberals, and specifically the First Amendment to the Constitution, erects a so-called "wall of separation between church and state" that cannot and must not be transgressed in anyway. Moreover, say liberals, the government cannot in any way support or favor religious faith.

This philosophy, this misreading of American history, this mistaken interpretation of our Constitution, has led to a relentless assault on America's religious institutions and traditions by our educational system, the courts and throughout our popular culture.

This little book, *One Nation Under God,* corrects the "Liberal History Lesson," and provides a powerful refutation to court rulings banning prayer from the schools, prohibiting the Ten Commandments from being posted in government buildings, and outlawing nativity scenes and other religious displays from public places.

And what has been the result of the relentless

assault on America's Christian heritage by our schools, universities and courts?

Certainly no one can deny the shocking moral decay we see all around us. Everywhere we look in secular society, traditional moral and religious values and beliefs are under attack: in the news media, on TV programs, and throughout our popular culture. Meanwhile, the Boy Scouts are under siege, pornography is easily accessible to kids, schools distribute condoms to children without the consent of parents. In schools today you can talk about "homoerotic" films and teach children how to put on a condom. But mention Jesus, and the anti-Christian mob will crack down hard.

And now that our schools have been wiped clean of Christian influence, efforts are underway by anti-Christian legal groups to completely "sanitize" our nation of any Christian references by,

* Removing "In God We Trust" from our currency.
* Ending opening each session of Congress
    with prayer.
* Ending Christmas as a national holiday.
* And eliminating the rank of military chaplain
    from our armed services.

*One Nation Under God* sets the record straight about America's Christian heritage — a Christian heritage that gave us all the civil liberties Americans now enjoy. This little book proves, beyond any doubt, that America was founded predominantly by Bible-believing Christians, that America's political institutions were constructed entirely upon Christian principles, and that America's Founding Fathers had in mind a government that would not only be hospitable toward Christianity, but would actively encourage and promote Christianity and reverence for God. As the United States Supreme Court stated so clearly in 1892:

Our laws and our institutions must necessarily be based upon the teachings of the redeemer of mankind. It is impossible that it should be otherwise; and in this sense and to the extent, our civilization and our institutions are emphatically Christian.

*One Nation Under God* is chock full of powerful and compelling statements by America's Founding Fathers, American Presidents, great American statesmen, in addition to Supreme Court rulings and proclamations by Congress on the all-important role of the Christian faith in building our great nation.

The quotations are alphabetically arranged for easy reference.

We believe *One Nation Under God* will prove to be an indispensable reference for Christian teachers, students politicians, lawmakers, and school boards. The quotations and statements contained in this little volume can be used for journalism articles, letters to editors, school and college reports, communications to elected officials, and in conversions with your friends and loved ones.

We are currently printing and distributing millions of copies of this little book to school children, college students, teachers, school principals, parents, college professors and politicians across America because we believe a clear presentation of the facts is our best strategy to show that America's faith in God was the key reason America grew to become a great nation.

*Benjamin Hart*
*President*
*Christian Defense Fund*

# JOHN ADAMS

John Adams was America's second President, George Washington's Vice President, a signer of the Declaration of Independence, and a member of the Continental Congress. He also authored the classic three-volume work titled, *A Defense of the Constitutions of the Government of the United States.* It was Adams who urged Thomas Jefferson to draft the Declaration of Independence. It was Adams who recommended that Congress appoint George Washington to be Commander-in-Chief of the Continental Army. And it was Adams who negotiated the final treaty with Great Britain ending the Revolutionary War.

In his diary entry dated February 22, 1756, John Adams wrote:

> *Suppose a nation in some distant region should take the Bible for their only law book, and every member should regulate his conduct by the precepts there exhibited! Every member would be obliged in conscience, to temperance, frugality, and industry; to justice, kindness, and charity towards his fellow men; and to piety, love and reverence toward Almighty God...What a Utopia, what a Paradise would this region be.*

On July 1, 1776, John Adams declared before the Continental Congress, as the 13 colonies were getting ready to sever ties from Great Britain:

> *Before God, I believe the hour has come. My judgement approves this measure, and my whole heart is in it. All that I have, and all that I am, and all that I hope in this life, I am now ready here to stake upon it. And I leave off as I began, that live or die, survive or perish, I am for the Declaration. It is my living sentiment, and by the blessing of God it shall be my dying sentiment. Independence now, and Independence for ever!*

On July 3, 1776, John Adams made this statement, regarding America's decision the previous day to declare independence from Great Britain:

> *The second day of July, 1776, will be the most memorable epoch in the history of America, to be celebrated by succeeding generations as the great anniversary festival, commemorated as the day of deliverance by solemn acts of devotion to God Almighty from one end of the Continent to the other, from this time forward forevermore.*

# SAMUEL ADAMS

Known as the "Father of the American Revolution," Sam Adams organized the famous Boston Tea Party, a landmark event that sparked the War of Independence with Great Britain. He also formed the "Committees of Correspondence" which organized the colonists to actively resist the authority of the British Government. A cousin of John Adams, Sam Adams was a signer of the Declaration of Independence and called the first Continental Congress. He served in the Congress until 1781. Adams was a steadfast Christian. In his work, *The Rights of the Colonists,* which was circulated in 1772, Adams boldly asserted:

> *The right to freedom being the gift of the Almighty...The rights of the colonists as Christians...may be best understood by reading and carefully studying the institutions of The Great Law Giver and Head of the Christian Church, which are to be found clearly written and promulgated in the New Testament.*

As the Declaration of Independence was being signed in 1776, Sam Adams declared:

> *We have this day restored the Sovereign to Whom all men ought to be obedient. He reigns*

*in Heaven and from the rising to the setting of
the sun, let His kingdom come.*

And Adams wrote these poignant words in his Last
Will and Testament:

*Principally, and first of all, I resign my soul to
the Almighty Being who gave it, and my body I
commit to the dust, relying on the merits of
Jesus Christ for the pardon of my sins.*

# THE CONTINENTAL CONGRESS

The Continental Congress of the original 13
colonies of what would become the United States of
America was established to resist the unfair tax
practices and tyrannical laws and policies imposed on
the colonies by Great Britain. On September 6, 1774 —
less than two years before the colonies formally
declared independence from Great Britain — the
Continental Congress made its first official act a call for
prayer. And on May 16, 1776, the Continental
Congress appointed an official national day of fasting
and prayer for the colonies:

*The Congress....Desirous...to have people of all*

*ranks and degrees duly impressed with a
solemn sense of God's superintending
providence, and of their duty, devoutly to
rely...on His aid and direction...Do earnestly
recommend Friday, the 17th day of May be
observed by the colonies as a day of
humiliation, fasting, and prayer; that we may,
with united hearts, confess and bewailed our
manifold sins and transgressions, and, by
sincere repentance and amendment of life,
appease God's righteous displeasure, and,
through the merits and mediation of Jesus
Christ, obtain this pardon and forgiveness.*

The Continental Congress on September 11, 1777,
ordered the importation of 20,000 Bibles for the
American troops. The law read as follows:

*The use of the Bible is so universal and its
importance so great that your committee refers
the above to the consideration of Congress, and
if Congress shall not think it expedient to order
the importation of types and paper, the
Committee recommends that Congress will
order the Committee of Commerce to import
20,000 Bibles from Holland, Scotland, or
elsewhere, into the different parts of the States
of the Union.*

*Whereupon it was resolved accordingly to direct said Committee of Commerce to import 20,000 copies of the Bible.*

Indeed, the Congress authorized its endorsement to be printed on the front page of the edition of the Bible approved for the American people:

*Whereupon, Resolved, that the Unites States in Congress assembled...recommend this edition of the Bible to the inhabitants of the Unites States, and hereby authorize [Robert Aitken] to publish this recommendation in the manner he shall think proper.*

The Continental Congress on October 18, 1780, issued another Proclamation for a Day of Public Thanksgiving and Prayer:

*Whereas it hath pleased Almighty God, the Father of all mercies, amidst the vicissitudes and calamities of war, to bestow blessings on the people of these states, which call for their devout and thankful acknowledgments, more especially in the late remarkable interposition of his watchful providence, in the rescuing the person of our Commander-in-Chief and the army from imminent dangers, at the moment when treason was ripened for execution...*

*It is therefore recommended to the several states...a day of public thanksgiving and prayer, that all the people may assemble on that day celebrate the praises of our Divine Benefactor; to confess our unworthiness of the least of His favors, and to offer our fervent supplication to the God of all grace...to cause the knowledge of Christianity to spread over all the earth.*

On July 13, 1787, the Continental Congress passed "An Ordinance for the Government of the Territory of the United States." This law was passed again by the United States Congress and signed into law by President George Washington on August 4, 1789:

*Article III*
*Religion, morality, and knowledge being necessary to good government and the happiness of mankind, schools and the means of education shall be forever encouraged.*

# CONGRESS OF THE UNITED STATES

When the War of Independence drew to a close, the Continental Congress became the Congress of the United States of America. On May 1, 1789, the U.S. House of Representatives voted to elect Reverend William Linn, a Dutch Reformed minister, as its chaplain. In addition, the Congress appropriated $500.00 from the federal treasury to pay his salary. The Right Reverend Bishop Samuel Provost was elected to be the chaplain of the Senate and was also paid from the federal treasury. Both the House and the Senate continue today to open each session with prayer. So much for the inviolate "wall of Separation of church and state" that anti-Christian organizations like the ACLU claim.

Indeed, on September 25, 1789, Congress unanimously approved a resolution asking President George Washington to proclaim a National Day of Thanksgiving:

> *Day of Thanksgiving. Resolved. That a joint committee of both Houses be directed to wait upon the President of the United States to request that he recommend to the people of the United States a day of public thanksgiving and*

*prayer, to be observed by acknowledging, with grateful hearts, the many signal favors of Almighty God, especially by affording them an opportunity peaceably to establish a constitution of government for their safety and happiness.*

# THE DECLARATION OF INDEPENDENCE

On July 4, 1776, the delegates to the Continental Congress formally declared our national independence from Great Britain. Here are the words of the Declaration of Independence:

*When in the Course of human events, it becomes necessary for one people to dissolve the political bands which have connected them with another, and to assume among the powers of the earth the separate and equal station to which the Laws of Nature and of Nature's God entitles them...*

*We hold these truths to be self-evident, that all men are created equal. That they are endowed by their Creator with certain unalienable rights, that among these are life, liberty and the pursuit of happiness...*

*We, Therefore, the Representatives of the
United States of America, in General Congress,
Assembled, appealing to the Supreme Judge of
the world for the rectitude of our intentions...*

*And for the support of this Declaration, with a
firm reliance on the protection of Divine
Providence, we mutually pledge to each other
our lives, our fortunes, and our sacred honor.*

# ALEXIS DE TOCQUEVILLE

Alexis de Tocqueville was the famous 19th century
French statesman, historian and social philosopher. He
traveled to America in the 1830s to discover the reasons
for the incredible success of this new nation. He
published his observations in his classic two-volume
work, Democracy in America. He was especially
impressed by America's religious character. Here are
some startling excerpts from Tocqueville's great work:

*Upon my arrival in the United States the
religious aspect of the country was the first
thing that struck my attention; and the longer I
stayed there, the more I perceived the great*

*political consequences resulting from this new state of things.*

*In France I had almost always seen the spirit of religion and the spirit of freedom marching in opposite directions. But in America I found they were intimately united and that they reigned in common over the same country. Religion in America...must be regarded as the foremost of the political institutions of that country; for if it does not impart a taste for freedom, it facilitates the use of it. Indeed, it is in this same point of view that the inhabitants of the United States themselves look upon religious belief.*

*I do not know whether all Americans have a sincere faith in their religion — for who can search the human heart? But I am certain that they hold it to be indispensable to the maintenance of republican institutions. This opinion is not peculiar to a class of citizens or a party, but it belongs to the whole nation and to every rank of society.*

*In the United States, the sovereign authority is religious...there is no country in the world where the Christian religion retains a greater influence over the souls of men than in America, and there can be no greater proof of its utility and of its conformity to human nature than that its influence is powerfully felt over the most enlightened and free nation of the earth.*

*In the United States, the influence of religion is not confined to the manners, but it extends to the intelligence of the people...*

*Christianity, therefore, reigns without obstacle, by universal consent...*

*I sought for the key to the greatness and genius of America in her harbors...; in her fertile fields and boundless forests; in her rich mines and vast world commerce; in her public school system and institutions of learning. I sought for it in her democratic Congress and in her matchless Constitution.*

*Not until I went into the churches of America and heard her pulpits flame with righteousness did I understand the secret of her genius and power.*

*America is great because America is good, and if America ever ceases to be good, America will cease to be great.*

*The safeguard of morality is religion, and morality is the best security of law as well as the surest pledge of freedom.*

*The Americans combine the notions of Christianity and of liberty so intimately in their minds, that it is impossible to make them conceive the one without the other*

*Christianity is the companion of liberty in all its conflicts — the cradle of its infancy, and the divine source of its claims.*

Tocqueville gives this account of a court case in New York:

*While I was in America, a witness, who happened to be called at the assizes of the county of Chester (state of New York), declared that he did not believe in the existence of God or in the immortality of the soul. The judge refused to admit his evidence, on the ground that the witness had destroyed beforehand all confidence of the court in what he was about to say. The newspapers related the fact without any further comment. The New York Spectator of August 23rd, 1831, relates the fact in the following terms:*

> "*The court of common pleas of Chester county (New York), a few days since rejected a witness who declared his disbelief in the existence of God. The presiding judge remarked, that he had not before been aware that there was a man living who did not believe in the existence of God; that this belief constituted the sanction of all testimony in a court of justice: and that he knew of no case in a Christian country, where a witness had been permitted to testify without such belief.*"

# BENJAMIN FRANKLIN

Benjamin Franklin was one of America's most influential and famous founding fathers. He was also a scientist, and author and a printer. He founded the University of Pennsylvania, signed the Declaration of Independence and the Constitution of the United States, and was Governor of the state of Pennsylvania.

As Governor, Franklin in 1748 proposed a day of fasting and prayer for Pennsylvania:

*It is the duty of mankind on all suitable occasions to acknowledge their dependence on the Divine Being...[that] Almighty God would mercifully interpose and still the rage of war among the nations...[and that] He would take this province under His protection, confound the designs and defeat the attempts of its enemies, and unite our hearts and strengthen our hands in every undertaking that may be for the public good, and for our defense and security in this time of danger.*

Here are some noteworthy excerpts from Franklin's Autobiography:

*I have been religiously educated as a Presbyterian; and ... I was never without religious principles.*

*I never doubted, for instance, the existence of the Deity; that he made the world, and governed it by his Providence; that the most acceptable service of God was the doing good to man; that our souls are immortal; and that all crime will be punished, and virtue reward, either here or hereafter.*

*These I esteemed the essentials of every*

*religion; and, being to be found in all the*
*religions we had in our country, I respected*
*them all, though with different degrees of*
*respect, as I found them more or less mixed*
*with other articles, which without any tendency*
*to inspire, promote, or confirm morality, served*
*principally to divide us, and made us unfriendly*
*on one another.*

*This respect of all...induced me to avoid all*
*discourse that might tend to lessen the good*
*opinion another might have of his own religion;*
*and as our province increased in people, and*
*new places of worship were continually*
*wanted, and generally erected by voluntary*
*contribution, my mite for such purpose,*
*whatever might be the sect, was never refused.*

*Though I seldom attended any public worship,*
*I had still an opinion of its propriety, and of its*
*utility when rightly conducted, and I regularly*
*paid my annual subscription for the support of*
*the only Presbyterian minister or meeting we*
*had in Philadelphia. He used to visit me*
*sometimes as a friend, and admonish me to*
*attend his administration.*

In July of 1776, the Congress appointed Franklin to

a committee charted to develop a seal for the new United States of America — a seal that would capture the spirit and character of the new nation. This is what Franklin proposed:

> *Moses lifting up his wand, and dividing the Red Sea, and Pharaoh in his chariot overwhelmed with the waters. This motto: 'Rebellion to tyrants is obedience to God.'*

Here's what Franklin wrote in a letter dated March 1778 to the Ministry of France:

> *Whoever shall introduce into public affairs the principals of primitive Christianity will change the face of the world.*

In addition, Franklin wrote:

> *A Bible and a newspaper in every house, a good school in every district — all studied and appreciated as they merit — are the principal support of virtue, morality, and civil liberty.*

In a pamphlet titled *Information to Those Who Would Remove to America*, written for Europeans who were considering coming to America, Franklin made these observations:

*Hence bad examples to youth are more rare in
America, which must be a comfortable
consideration to parents. To this may be truly
added, that serious religion, under its various
denominations, is not only tolerated, but
respected and practiced.*

*Atheism is unknown there; infidelity rare and
secret; so that persons may live to a great age
in that country without having their piety
shocked by meeting with either an Atheist or an
Infidel.*

*And the Divine Being seems to have manifested
his approbation of the mutual forbearance and
kindness with which the different sects treat
each other; by the remarkable prosperity with
which he has been pleased to favor the whole
country.*

On June 28, 1787, the Constitutional Convention
was deadlocked and embroiled in bitter controversy.
Benjamin Franklin rose and made the following plea to
the delegates:

*In the beginning of the Contest with Great
Britain, when we were sensible of danger, we*

*had daily prayer in this room for the Divine protection. Our prayers, Sir, were heard, and they were graciously answered. All of us who were engaged in the struggle must have observed frequent instances of a superintending providence in our favor.*

*To that kind providence we owe this happy opportunity of consulting in peace on the means of establishing our future national felicity. And have we now forgotten that powerful Friend? Or do we imagine we no longer need His assistance?*

*I have lived, Sir, a long time, and the longer I live, the more convincing proofs I see of this truth — that God governs in the affairs of men. And if a sparrow cannot fall to the ground without His notice, is it probable that an empire can rise without His aid?*

*We have been assured, Sir, in the Sacred Writings, that 'except the Lord build the House, they labor in vain that build it.' I firmly believe this; and I also believe that without His concurring aid we shall succeed in this political building no better than the builders of Babel: We shall be divided by our partial local interests; our projects will be confounded, and we ourselves shall become a reproach and bye word down to future ages ...*

*I therefore beg leave to move — that henceforth prayers imploring the assistance of Heaven, and its blessing on our deliberations, be held in this Assembly every morning before we proceed to business, and that one or more of the clergy of this city be requested to officiate in that service.*

# ALEXANDER HAMILTON

Alexander Hamilton, a signer of the Constitution and one of America's most preeminent founding fathers, was author of 51 of the 85 Federalist Papers, which powerfully made the case for ratifying the Constitution. He was Secretary of the Treasury in George Washington's administration.  Shortly after the Constitutional Convention of 1787, Hamilton stated:

*For my own part, I sincerely esteem it a system which without the finger of God, never could have been suggested and agreed upon by such a diversity of interests.*

Alexander Hamilton regularly led his household in family prayer. He also wrote about the important connection between political freedom and Christianity:

> In my opinion, the present Constitution is the standard to which we are to cling. Under its banner bona fide must we combat our political foes, reflecting all changes but through the channel itself provided for amendments. By these general views of the subject have my reflections been guided.

> I now offer you the outline of the plan they have suggested. Let an association be formed to be denominated 'The Christian Constitutional Society,' its object to be First: The support of the Christian religion. Second: The support of the United States.

Alexander Hamilton further argued:

> I have carefully examined the evidences of the Christian religion, and if I was sitting as a juror upon its authenticity I would unhesitatingly give my verdict in its favor. I can prove its truth as clearly as any proposition ever submitted to the mind of man.

Hamilton was shot and killed by Aaron Burr in a

duel on July 12, 1804. Hamilton's last dying words
were:

> *I have a tender reliance on the mercy of the*
> *Almighty, through the merits of the Lord Jesus*
> *Christ. I am a sinner. I look to Him for mercy;*
> *pray for me.*

# PATRICK HENRY

A famous Revolutionary leader and orator, Patrick
Henry said "Give me liberty, or give me death" which
became the battle cry of the American Revolution. He
was a five-time Governor of Virginia. He once
declared:

> *It cannot be emphasized too strongly or too*
> *often that this great nation was founded, not by*
> *religionists, but by Christians; not on religions,*
> *but on the Gospel of Jesus Christ.  For this very*
> *reason peoples of other faiths have been*
> *afforded asylum, prosperity, and freedom of*
> *worship here.*

On another occasion he said, pointing to his Bible:

> *The Bible is worth all other books which have*

*ever been printed.*

On November 20, 1798, in his Last Will and Testament, Patrick Henry wrote:

> *This is all the inheritance I give to my dear family. The religion of Christ will give them one which will make them rich indeed.*

On his death bed, Patrick Henry said:

> *Doctor, I wish you to observe how real and beneficial the religion of Christ is to a man about to die....I am, however, much consoled by reflecting that the religion of Christ has, from its first appearance in the world, been attacked in vain by all the wits, philosophers, and wise ones, aided by every power of man, and its triumphs have been complete.*

# ANDREW JACKSON

The seventh President of the United States, Andrew Jackson was a victorious General winning the "Battle of New Orleans" in the War of 1812 as well as capturing Florida. Jackson was also a noted lawyer, U.S. Senator and Judge on the Tennessee Supreme

Court. Jackson, on September 11, 1834, wrote this in a
letter to his son:

> *I nightly offer up my prayers to the throne of*
> *grace for the health and safety of you all, and*
> *that we ought all to rely with confidence on the*
> *promises of our dear Redeemer, and give Him*
> *our hearts. This is all He requires and all that*
> *we can do, and if we sincerely do this, we are*
> *sure of salvation through his atonement.*

Jackson wrote this to comfort the family of a friend
who had recently died:

> *Rely on our dear Savior. He will be father to*
> *the fatherless and husband to the widow. Trust*
> *in the mercy and goodness of Christ, and*
> *always be ready to say with heartfelt*
> *resignation, 'may the Lord's will be done.'*

Jackson wrote this in a letter on March 25, 1835:

> *I was brought up a rigid Presbyterian, to which*
> *I have always adhered. Our excellent*
> *Constitution guarantees to every one freedom*
> *of religion, and charity tells us (and you know*
> *Charity is the real basis of all true*
> *religion)...judge the tree by its fruit.*

*All who profess Christianity believe in a Savior, and that by and through Him we must be saved. We ought, therefore, to consider all good Christians whose walks correspond with their professions, be they Presbyterian, Episcopalian, Baptist, Methodist or Roman Catholic.*

Jackson wrote this in a letter to his wife:

*I trust that the God of Isaac and of Jacob will protect you, and give you health in my absence. In Him alone we ought to trust; He alone can preserve and guide us through this troublesome world, and I am sure He will hear your prayers. We are told that the prayers of the righteous prevaileth much, and I add mine for your health and preservation until we meet again.*

# THOMAS JEFFERSON

Thomas Jefferson was the primary author of the Declaration of Independence and was America's third President. He was a noted author, educator, architect and scientist. He founded the University of Virginia. In his Notes on the State of Virginia, he made this statement:

> *God who gave us life gave us liberty. And can*
> *the liberties of a nation be thought secure when*
> *we have removed their only firm basis, a*
> *conviction in the minds of the people that these*
> *liberties are of the gift of God? That they are*
> *not to be violated but with His wrath? Indeed, I*
> *tremble for my country when I reflect that God*
> *is just; that His justice cannot sleep forever.*

In a letter dated March 23, 1801, Jefferson wrote:

> *The Christian Religion, when divested of the*
> *rags in which they [the clergy] have enveloped*
> *it, and brought to the original purity and*
> *simplicity of its Benevolent Institutor, is a*
> *religion of all others most friendly to liberty,*
> *science, and the freest expansion of the human*
> *mind.*

In a letter to the Danbury Baptist Association of
Danbury, Connecticut, dated January 1, 1802, Jefferson
reassured the Baptists that the First Amendment to the
Constitution guaranteed them protection from
government oppression and interference:

> *Believing with you that religion is a matter*

*which lies solely between man and his God, that he owes account to none other for faith or his worship, that the legislative powers of government reach actions only, and not opinions, I contemplate with solemn reverence that act of the whole American people which declared that their legislature should 'make no law respecting an establishment of religion, or prohibiting the free exercise thereof,' thus building a wall of separation between Church and State.*

On April 21, 1803, Jefferson wrote this to Dr. Benjamin Rush (also a signer of the Declaration of Independence):

*My views...are the result of a life of inquiry and reflection, and very different from the anti-Christian system imputed to me by those who know nothing of my opinions. To the corruptions of Christianity I am, indeed, opposed; but not to the genuine precepts of Jesus himself. I am a Christian in the only sense in which He wished any one to be; sincerely attached to his doctrines in preference to all others...*

President Thomas Jefferson extended three times a

1787 act of Congress in which special lands were designated ...

> *... for the sole use of Christian Indians and the*
> *Moravian Brethren missionaries for civilizing*
> *the Indians and promoting Christianity.*

# ABRAHAM LINCOLN

After the Union army was defeated at the Battle of Bull Run, President Abraham Lincoln declared a National Day of Prayer and Fasting:

> *It is fit and becoming in all people, at all times,*
> *to acknowledge and revere the Supreme*
> *Government of God; to bow in humble*
> *submission to His chastisement; to confess and*
> *deplore their sins and transgressions in the full*
> *conviction that the fear of the Lord is the*
> *beginning of wisdom; and to pray, with all*
> *fervency and contrition, for the pardon of their*
> *past offenses, and for a blessing upon their*
> *present and prospective action.*
> *And whereas when our own beloved country,*
> *once, by the blessings of God, united,*
> *prosperous and happy, is now afflicted with*
> *faction and civil war, it is peculiarly fit for us to*

> *recognize the hand of God in this terrible
> visitation, and in sorrowful remembrance of
> our own faults and crimes as a nation and as
> individuals, to humble ourselves before Him
> and to pray for His mercy...that the inestimable
> boon of civil and religious liberty, earned under
> His guidance and blessing by the labors and
> sufferings of our fathers, may be restored.*

After losing the Second Battle of Bull Run, Lincoln wrote his famous *Meditation on the Divine* Will:

> *The will of God prevails. In great contests each
> party claims to act in accordance with the will
> of God. Both may be, and one must be wrong.
> God can not be for and against the same thing
> at the same time. In the present civil war it is
> quite possible that God's purpose is something
> different from the purpose of either party —
> and yet the human instrumentalities, working
> just as they do, are of the best adaptation to
> effect His purpose.*

> *I am almost ready to say this is probably true
> — that God wills this contest, and wills that it
> shall not end yet. By His mere quiet power, on
> the minds of the now contestants, He could
> have either saved or destroyed the Union*

*without a human contest. Yet the contest began.
And having begun He could give the final
victory to either side any day. Yet the contest
proceeds.*

President Lincoln is quoted making this statement
to Eliza Gurney on October 6, 1862:

> *If I had my way, this war would never have
> been commenced. If I had been allowed my
> way, this war would have ended before this. But
> we find it still continues; and we must believe
> that He permits it for some wise purpose of His
> own, mysterious and unknown to us; and
> though with our limited understanding we may
> not be able to comprehend it, yet we cannot but
> believe, that He who made the world still
> governs it.*

> *We are indeed going through a great trial — a
> fiery trial. In the very responsible position in
> which I happened to be placed, being a humble
> instrument in the hands of our Heavenly
> Father, as I am, and as we all are, to work out
> His great purposes, I have desired that all my
> works and acts may be according to His will,
> and that it might be so, I have sought His aid.*

Near the end of 1862, Lincoln made this tremendous statement to Reverend Byron Sunderland:

> *The ways of God are mysterious and profound beyond all comprehension — 'Who by searching can find Him out?' God only knows the issue of this business. He has destroyed nations from the map of history for their sins. Nevertheless, my hopes prevail generally above my fears for our Republic. The times are dark, the spirits of ruin are abroad in all their power, and the mercy of God alone can save us.*

Here is the text of Lincoln's Proclamation Appointing a National Fast Day, issued March 30, 1863:

> *Whereas, the Senate of the United States devoutly recognizing the Supreme Authority and just Government of Almighty God in all the affairs of men and of nations, has, by a resolution, requested the President to designate and set apart a day for national prayer and humiliation:*
>
> *And whereas, it is the duty of nations as well as of men to own their dependence upon the overruling power of God, to confess their sins*

*and transgressions in humble sorrow yet with
assured hope that genuine repentance will lead
to mercy and pardon, and to recognize the
sublime truth, announced in the Holy
Scriptures and proven by all history: that those
nations only are blessed whose God is Lord:*

*And, insomuch as we know that, by His divine
law, nations like individuals are subjected to
punishments and chastisement in this world,
may we not justly fear that the awful calamity
of civil war, which now desolates the land, may
be but a punishment inflicted upon us for our
presumptuous sins to the needful end of our
national reformation as a whole people?*

*We have been the recipients of the choicest
bounties of Heaven. We have been preserved
these many years in peace and prosperity. We
have grown in numbers, wealth and power as
no other nation has ever grown.*

*But we have forgotten God. We have forgotten
the gracious Hand which preserved us in
peace, and multiplied and enriched and
strengthened us; and we have vainly imagined,
in the deceitfulness of our hearts, that all these
blessings were produced by some superior*

*wisdom and virtue of our own.*

*Intoxicated with unbroken success, we have become too self-sufficient to feel the necessity of redeeming and preserving grace, too proud to pray to the God that made us!*

*It behooves us then to humble ourselves before the offended Power, to confess our national sins and to pray for clemency and forgiveness.*

*Now, therefore, in compliance with the request and fully concurring in the view of the Senate, I do, by this proclamation, designate and set apart Thursday, the 30th day of April, 1863, as a day of national humiliation, fasting and prayer.*

*And I do hereby request all the people to abstain on that day from their ordinary secular pursuits, and to unite, at their several places of public worship and their respective homes, in keeping the day holy to the Lord and devoted to the humble discharge of the religious duties proper to that solemn occasion.*

*All this being done, in sincerity and truth, let us then rest humbly in the hope authorized by the*

*Divine teachings, that the united cry of the
nation will be hard on high and answered with
blessing no less than the pardon of our national
sins and the restoration of our now divided and
suffering country to its former happy condition
of unity and peace.*

*In witness whereof, I have hereunto set my
hand and caused the seal of the United States
to be affixed. By the President: Abraham
Lincoln.*

Lincoln remained steadfast in his faith even when
General Robert E. Lee led his army of 76,000 men into
Pennsylvania. He explained to a general wounded at
Gettysburg:

*When everyone seemed panic-stricken...I went
to my room...and got down on my knees before
Almighty God and prayed...Soon a sweet
comfort crept into my soul that God Almighty
had taken the whole business into His own
hands...*

On November 19, 1863, Lincoln delivered his
famous Gettysburg Address. The entire speech is only
267 words and is engraved on the Lincoln Memorial in
Washington, D.C. In it, he talks about America as a

nation under God:

> *Fourscore and seven years ago our fathers
> brought forth upon this continent a new nation,
> conceived in liberty, and dedicated to the
> proposition that all men are created equal. Now
> we are engaged in a great civil war, testing
> whether that nation, or any nation so conceived
> and so dedicated, can long endure.*
>
> *We are met on a great battlefield of that war.
> We have come to dedicate a portion of that field
> as a final resting place for those who here gave
> their lives that that nation might live. It is
> altogether fitting and proper that we should do
> this.*
>
> *But in a larger sense we cannot dedicate, we
> cannot consecrate, we cannot hallow this
> ground. The brave men, living and dead, who
> struggled here, have consecrated it far above
> our poor power to add or detract.*
>
> *The world will little note, nor long remember,
> what we say here, but it can never forget what
> they did here. It is for us, the living, rather to be
> dedicated here to the unfinished work which
> they who fought here have thus far so nobly
> advanced.*

*It is rather for us to be here dedicated to the great task remaining before us — that from these honored dead we take increased devotion to that cause for which they gave the last full measure of devotion — that we here highly resolve that these dead shall not have died in vain — that this nation, under God, shall have a new birth of freedom — and that government of the people, by the people, for the people, shall not perish from the earth.*

During the war, Lincoln overheard someone remark that he hoped "the Lord was on the Union's side." Lincoln responded with this sharp rebuke:

*I am not at all concerned about that, for I know that the Lord is always on the side of the right. But it is my constant anxiety and prayer that I and this nation should be on the Lord's side.*

On September 5, 1864, the Committee of Colored People from Baltimore presented Lincoln with a Bible. Here's what Lincoln told them in his speech:

*In regard to this Great Book, I have but to say, I believe the Bible is the best gift God has given to man. All the good Savior gave to the world was communicated through this Book. But for*

*this Book we could not know right from wrong.
All things most desirable for man's welfare,
here and hereafter, are to be found portrayed in
it. To you I return my most sincere thanks for
the elegant copy of the great Book of God
which you present.*

# JAMES MADISON

James Madison is known as the father of the U.S.
Constitution. He was also the fourth President of the
United States. He was the primary author of the Bill of
Rights and engineered the Louisiana Purchase of 1803.
Madison believed Christianity to be the foundation
upon which a just government must be built. Writing on
June 20, 1785, he stated:

*Religion [is] the basis and Foundation of
Government.*

Madison expounds further:

*We have staked the whole future of American
civilization, not upon the power of government,
far from it. We have staked the future of all of
our political institutions upon the capacity of
mankind for self-government; upon the
capacity of each and all of us to govern*

*ourselves, to control ourselves, to sustain
ourselves according to the Ten Commandments
of God.*

In 1788, Madison stated:

*The belief in God all powerful wise and good,
is so essential to the moral order of the world
and to the happiness of man, that arguments
which enforce it cannot be drawn from too
many sources nor adapted with too much
solicitude to the different characters and
capacities to be impressed with it.*

In Madison's personal Bible, his hand written notes
appear in the margin of Chapter 19 of the Book of Acts:

*Believers who are in a state of grace, have
need of the Word of God for their edification
and building up therefore implies a possibility
of falling. v. 32.*

*Grace, it is the free gift of God. Luke. 12. 32-
v.32.*

*Giver more blessed than the receiver. v. 35.*

*To neglect the means for our own preservation*

*is to tempt God: and to trust to them is to neglect Him. v. 3 & Ch. 27. v. 31.*

*Humility, the better any man is, the lower thoughts he has of himself. v. 19.*
*Ministers to take heed to themselves & their flock. v. 28.*

*The Apostles did greater miracles than Christ, in the matter, not manner, of them. v. 11.*

In his manuscripts on the Gospels and the Acts of the Apostles, Madison wrote:

*Christ's Divinity appears by St. John, chapter xx, 2: 'And Thomas answered and said unto Him, my Lord and my God!' Resurrection testified to and witnessed by the Apostles, Acts iv, 33: 'And with great power gave the Apostles witness of the resurrection of the Lord Jesus, and great grace was upon them all.'*

On November 9, 1772, Madison wrote to his close college friend, William Bradford:

*A watchful eye must be kept on ourselves lest while we are building ideal monuments of renown and bliss here we neglect to have our names enrolled in the annals of Heaven.*

*[Bad health has] intimated to me not to expect
a long or healthy life, yet it may be better with
me after some time tho I hardly dare expect it
and therefore have little spirit and alacrity to
set about anything that is difficult in acquiring
and useless in possessing after one has
exchanged time for eternity.*

# NORTHWEST ORDINANCE

Passed by Congress on July 13, 1787, the
Northwest Ordinance established laws, rules and
principles under which territories Northwest of the
Ohio River could be settled and incorporated into the
United States. An important goal of the Northwest
Ordinance was to spread Christianity to the Indian
tribes. The landmark law reads:

*SECTION 13.  And, for extending the
fundamental principles of civil and religious
liberty, which form the basis whereon these
republics, their laws and constitutions are
erected:*

*to fix and establish those principles as the basis*

of all laws, constitutions and governments, which forever hereafter shall be formed in the said territory:

to provide also for the establishment of states, and permanent government therein, and for their admission to a share in the federal councils on an equal footing with the original states, at as early period as my be consistent with the general interest:

SECTION 14. It is hereby ordained and declared by the authority aforesaid, that the following articles shall be considered as articles of compact, between the original states and the people and states of the said territory, and forever remain unalienable, unless by common consent, to wit:

ARTICLE I. No person, demeaning himself in a peaceable and orderly manner, shall ever be molested on account of his mode of worship or religious sentiments in the said territory...

ARTICLE III. Religion, morality, and knowledge being necessary to good government and the happiness of mankind, schools and the means of education shall forever be encouraged.

# THOMAS PAINE

As the author of the famous political pamphlet titled Common Sense, Thomas Paine helped fan the flames of the American Revolution. George Washington ordered the first essay from Common Sense read aloud to the troops at Valley Forge. Here's a noteworthy excerpt from Paine's essay:

> *Tyranny, like hell, is not easily conquered; yet we have this consolation with us, that the harder the conflict, the more glorious the triumph.*

> *What we obtain too cheaply, we esteem too lightly; 'tis dearness only that gives everything its value. Heaven knows how to put a price upon its goods; and it would be strange indeed if so celestial an article as freedom should not be highly rated.*

> *The cause of America is in a great measure the cause of all mankind. Where, say some, is the king of America? I'll tell you, friend, He reigns above.*

> *Yet that we may not appear to be defective even*

*in earthly honors, let a day be solemnly set
apart for proclaiming the charter; let it be
placed on the Divine Law, the Word of God; let
a crown be placed thereon.*

*The Almighty implanted in us these
inextinguishable feelings for good and wise
purposes. They are the guardians of His image
in our heart. They distinguish us from the herd
of common animals.*

Paine later became infatuated with the French
Revolution, which he mistakenly saw as in the same
tradition as the American Revolution. Paine later
realized his error. The American Revolution was based
on Christian principles, while the French Revolution
was hostile to Christianity. The American Revolution
resulted in unprecedented political liberty for its
citizens, while the French Revolution ended in a
bloodthirsty tyranny. Paine's unfortunate defense of the
French Revolution was titled The Age of Reason, a
book he later recanted:

*I would give worlds, if I had them, if The Age
of Reason had never been published. O Lord,
help! Stay with me! It is hell to be left alone.*

Thomas Paine's last words were:

> *I die in perfect composure and resignation to the will of my Creator, God.*

# PRINCETON UNIVERSITY

Founded in 1746 by Presbyterians, Princeton was originally named 'The College of New Jersey.' For the first century and a half — up until 1902 — every President of Princeton had been a minister. Princeton's most famous President was Jonathan Edwards, America's greatest theologian, as well as a prolific author and influential preacher. The University's official motto was:

> *Under God's Power She Flourishes.*

Princeton's first President, the Reverend Jonathan Dickinson, declared:

> *Cursed be all that learning that is contrary to the cross of Christ.*

# JOHN ROBINSON

John Robinson was pastor of the Pilgrim Church in England and Holland, before their departure to America in the Mayflower. On July 22, 1620, Robinson gave this word of warning to the Pilgrims as they were getting ready to sail to the New World:

> *Lastly, whereas you are become a body politic, using amongst yourselves civil government, let your wisdom and godliness appear not only in choosing such persons as do entirely love and will promote the common good but also in yielding unto them all due honor and obedience in their lawful administrations; not beholding in them the ordinariness of their persons, but God's ordinance for your good...*

> *Someone or few must be appointed over the assembly [for]...discussing and determining of all matters, so in this royal assembly, the church of Christ, though all be Kings, yet some most faithful and most able, are to be set over the rest...wherein...they are...charged to minister according to the Testament of Christ.*

In a famous letter to the Mayflower Pilgrims, Robinson wrote:

> *Thus this holy army of saints is marshaled here on earth by these officers, under the conduct of their glorious Emperor, Christ. Thus it marches*

*in this most heavenly order and gracious array,
against all enemies, both bodily and ghostly:
peaceable in itself, as Jerusalem, terrible too
the enemy as an army with banners, triumphing
over their tyranny with patience, their cruelty
with meekness and over death itself with dying.*

*Thus, through the Blood of that spotless Lamb,
and that Word of their testimony, they are more
than conquerors, bruising the head of the
Serpent; yea, through the power of His Word,
they have power to cast down Satan like
lightning; to tread upon serpents and
scorpions; to cast down strongholds, and
everything that exalteth itself against God.*

*The gates of Hell, and all the principalities and
powers on earth, shall not prevail against it.
Romans 12; I Corinthians 12; Revelation 14:1,
2; Song 6:3; Revelation 12:11; Luke 10:18, 19;
2 Corinthians 10:15; Matthew 16:18, Romans
8:38, 39...*

# JOSEPH STORY

A Congressman and Professor of Law at Harvard,
Joseph Story was appointed to the Supreme Court in

1811 by James Madison, the Father of the U.S.
Constitution. He served on the Court for 34 years.
Story's great work, *Commentaries on the Constitution
of the United States,* is considered a classic of American
jurisprudence. He was instrumental in establishing the
illegality of the slave trade. He also convincingly
argued that the United States of America was built on
the principles of Christianity. In a speech at Harvard,
Story stated bluntly:

> *There never has been a period of history, in
> which the Common Law did not recognize
> Christianity as lying at its foundation.*

In his work, *A Familiar Exposition of the
Constitution of the United States,* Justice Story, had this
to say about the purpose the First Amendment:

> *We are not to attribute this prohibition of a
> national religious establishment [in the First
> Amendment] to an indifference to religion in
> general, and especially to Christianity (which
> none could hold in more reverence than the
> framers of the Constitution)....*

> *Probably, at the time of the adoption of the
> Constitution, and of the Amendment to it now
> under consideration, the general, if not the*

> *universal, sentiment in America was, that*
> *Christianity ought to receive encouragement*
> *from the State so far as was not incompatible*
> *with the private rights of conscience and the*
> *freedom of religious worship.*

> *Any attempt to level all religions, and to make*
> *it a matter of state policy to hold all in utter*
> *indifference, would have created universal*
> *disapprobation, if not universal indignation.*

In other words, the purpose of the First Amendment
was to protect a religious people from the government
— not to protect the government from a religious
people. It is perfectly all right, under the First
Amendment, for the Government of the United States
to favor Christianity over other faiths — so long as
other faiths are not persecuted by the government, and
so long as the national government does not attempt to
set up a national church, such as the Anglican Church
in England. In his *Commentaries on the Constitution*,
Justice Story stated:

> *It yet remains a problem to be solved in human*
> *affairs, whether any free government can be*
> *permanent where the public worship of God,*
> *and the support of religion, constitute no part*
> *of the policy or duty of the state in any*

*assignable shape.*

In fact, in his commentary on the purpose of First Amendment, Justice Story stated:

> *The real object of the First Amendment was not to countenance much less to advance Mohammedanism, or Judaism, or infidelity, by prostrating Christianity, but to exclude all rivalry among Christian sects [denominations] and to prevent any national ecclesiastical patronage of the national government.*

# NOTEWORTHY DECISIONS CONCERNING RELIGION BY THE SUPREME COURT OF THE UNITED STATES

*1844, Vidal v. Girard's Executors, 43 U.S. 126,132.*

Lawyers speaking for the City of Philadelphia, which opposed the establishment of a Deist school by a Frenchman named Stephen Girard, argued:

> *The plan of education proposed is anti-*

*Christian, and therefore repugnant to the law....The purest principles of morality are to be taught. Where are they found? Whoever searches for them must go to the source from which a Christian man derives his faith — the Bible...There is an obligation to teach what the Bible alone can teach, viz. a pure system of morality...*

*Both in the Old and New Testaments [religious instruction's] importance is recognized. In the Old it is said, 'Thou shalt diligently teach them to thy children,' and the New, 'Suffer the little children to come unto me and forbid them not...' No fault can be found with Girard for wishing a marble college to bear his name forever, but it is not valuable unless it has a fragrance of Christianity about it.*

The United States Supreme Court agreed, and in a unanimous opinion read by Justice Joseph Story ruled as follows:

*Christianity...is not to be maliciously and openly reviled and blasphemed against, to the annoyance of believers or the injury of the public...It is unnecessary for us, however, to consider the establishment of a school or college, for the propagation of...Deism, or any other form of infidelity.*

*Such a case is not to be presumed to exist in a Christian country...Why may not laymen instruct in the general principles of Christianity as well as ecclesiastics...*

*And we cannot overlook the blessings, which such [lay] men by their conduct, as well as their instructions, may, nay must, impart to their youthful pupils. Why may not the Bible, and especially the New Testament, without note or comment, be read and taught as a divine revelation in the [school] — its general precepts expounded, its evidences explained and its glorious principles of morality inculcated?...*

*Where can the purest principles of morality be learned so clearly or so perfectly as from the New Testament?*

*It is also said, and truly, that the Christian religion is a part of the common law of Pennsylvania...*

**1890, The United States v. the Church of Jesus Christ of Latter Day Saints v. United States, 136 U.S.**

The U.S. Supreme Court ruled that polygamy could not be practiced in the United States, stating that:

> *It is contrary to the spirit of Christianity and*
> *the civilization which Christianity has*
> *produced in the Western world.*

### 1892, Church of the Holy Trinity v. United States.

This powerful ruling by the U.S. Supreme Court chronicles Christianity's central role in shaping America's political institutions and traditions:

> *Our laws and our institutions must necessarily*
> *be based upon and embody the teachings of the*
> *Redeemer of mankind. It is impossible that it*
> *should be otherwise; and in this sense and to*
> *this extent our civilization and our institutions*
> *are emphatically Christian.*
>
> *No purpose of action against religion can be*
> *imputed to any legislation, state or national,*
> *because this is a religious people. This is*
> *historically true. From the discovery of this*
> *continent to the present hour, there is a single*
> *voice making this affirmation.*

*The commission to Christopher Columbus...[recited] that 'it is hoped that by God's assistance some of the continents and islands in the ocean will be discovered...'*

*The first colonial grant made to Sir Walter Raleigh in 1584...and the grant authorizing him to enact statutes for the government of the proposed colony provided that they 'be not against the true Christian faith...'*

*The first charter of Virginia, granted by King James I in 1606...commenced the grant in these words: '...in propagating of Christian religion to such people as yet live in darkness...'*

*Language of similar import may be found in the subsequent charters of that colony...in 1609 and 1611; and the same is true of the various charters granted to the other colonies. In language more or less emphatic is the establishment of the Christian religion declared to be one of the purposes of the grant. The celebrated compact made by the Pilgrims in the Mayflower, 1620, recites: 'Having undertaken for the Glory of God, and advancement of the Christian faith...a voyage to plant the first colony in the northern parts of Virginia...'*

*The Fundamental Orders of Connecticut, under which a provisional government was instituted in 1638-1639, commence with this declaration: 'And well knowing where a people are gathered together, the Word of God requires that to maintain the peace and union...there should be an orderly and decent government established according to God...to maintain and preserve the liberty and purity of the Gospel of our Lord Jesus which we now profess...of the said Gospel [which] is now practiced amongst us.'*

*In the Charter of Privileges granted by William Penn to the province of Pennsylvania, in 1701, it is recited: '...No people can be truly happy, though under the greatest enjoyment of civil liberties, if abridged of...their religious profession and worship...'*

*Coming nearer to the present time, the Declaration of Independence recognizes the presence of the Divine in human affairs in these words:*

*'We hold these truths to be self-evident, that all men are created equal, that they are endowed by their Creator with certain unalienable*

*rights...appealing to the Supreme Judge of the world for the rectitude of our intentions...And for the support of this Declaration, with firm reliance on the Protection of Divine Providence, we mutually pledge to each other our lives, our fortunes, and our sacred honor.'*

*We find everywhere a clear recognition of the same truth...because of a general recognition of this truth [that we are a Christian nation], the question has seldom been presented to the courts...*

*There is no dissonance in these declarations. There is a universal language pervading them all, having one meaning; they affirm and reaffirm that this is a religious nation. These are not individual sayings, declarations of private persons: they are organic utterances; they speak the voice of the entire people.*

*While because of a general recognition of this truth the question has seldom been presented to the courts, yet we find that in Updegraph v. the Commonwealth, it was decided that, Christianity, general Christianity, is, and always has been, a part of the common law...not Christianity with an established*

*church...but Christianity with liberty of
conscience to all men.*

*And in The People v. Ruggles, Chancellor
Kent, the great commentator on American law,
speaking as Chief Justice of the Supreme Court
of New York, said: 'The people of this State, in
common with the people of this country, profess
the general doctrines of Christianity, as the rule
of their faith and practice...We are a Christian
people, and the morality of the country is
deeply engrafted upon Christianity, and not
upon the doctrines or worship of those
impostors [other religions].'*

*And in the famous case of Vidal v. Girard's
Executors, this court observed: 'It is also said,
and truly, that the Christian religion is a part of
the common law...'*

*If we pass beyond these matters to a view of
American life as expressed by its laws, its
business, its customs and its society, we find
everywhere a clear recognition of the same
truth. Among other matters note the following:
The form of oath universally prevailing,
concluding with an appeal to the Almighty; the
custom of opening sessions of all deliberative*

*bodies and most conventions with prayer; the prefatory words of all will, 'In the name of God, amen', the laws respecting the observance of the Sabbath, with the general cessation of all secular business, and the closing of courts, legislatures, and other similar public assemblies on that day; the churches and church organizations which abound in every city, town and hamlet; the multitude of charitable organizations existing everywhere under Christian auspices; the gigantic missionary associations, with general support, and aiming to establish Christian missions in every quarter of the globe.*

*These, and many other matters which might be noticed, add a volume of unofficial declarations to the mass of organic utterances that this is a Christian nation...we find everywhere a clear recognition of the same truth.*

*The happiness of a people and the good order and preservation of civil government essentially depend upon piety, religion and morality.*

*Religion, morality, and knowledge [are] necessary to good government, the preservation of liberty, and the happiness of mankind.*

## 1948, McCollum v. Board of Education

In this powerful ruling, the Supreme Court defined the crucial and central role of Christianity in the history of American education:

> *Traditionally, organized education in the*
> *Western world was Church education. It could*
> *hardly be otherwise when the education of*
> *children was primarily study of the Word and*
> *the ways of God. Even in the Protestant*
> *countries, where there was a less close*
> *identification of Church and State, the basis of*
> *education was largely the Bible, and its chief*
> *purpose inculcation of piety.*

## 1952, Zorach v. Clauson

In this important ruling, the Supreme Court clearly defined the meaning of the First Amendment and the doctrine of "Separation of Church and State." The purpose of the First Amendment is merely to prohibit the establishment of an official national church, similar to England's Anglican Church. The Founding Fathers were not trying to prohibit the federal government from supporting religious institutions, promoting a reverence for God, or even favoring Christianity over other religious faiths. According to the Supreme Court's ruling:

> *The First Amendment, however, does not say that in every respect there shall be a separation of Church and State. Rather, it studiously defines the manner, the specific ways, in which there shall be no concert or union or dependency one on the other.*

> *That is the common sense of the matter. Otherwise the state and religion would be aliens to each other — hostile, suspicious, and even unfriendly.*

# GEORGE WASHINGTON

The father of our nation was quiet about his Christian faith. But there can be no doubt his faith in our Lord Jesus Christ was deep and heartfelt. In his first general order to his troops, General George Washington called on ...

> *Every officer and man...to live, and act, as*

*becomes a Christian Soldier defending the*
*dearest rights and liberties of his country.*

On May 14, 1787, George Washington warned the
delegates to the Constitutional Convention:

*If to please the people, we offer what we*
*ourselves disapprove, how can we afterward*
*defend our work?  Let us raise a standard to*
*which the wise and the honest can repair; the*
*event is in the Hand of God!*

President George Washington, on April 30, 1789,
delivered his famous Inaugural Address to both Houses
of Congress. He had just taken the oath of office on the
balcony of Federal Hall in New York City, with his
hand upon a Bible opened to Deuteronomy, Chapter 28:

*Such being the impressions under which I have,*
*in obedience to the public summons, repaired*
*to the present station, it would be peculiarly*
*improper to omit, in this first official act, my*
*fervent supplications to that Almighty Being*
*who rules over the universe, who presides in*
*the councils of nations and whose providential*
*aides can supply every human defect; that His*
*benediction may consecrate to the liberties and*
*happiness of the people of the United States a*

*government instituted by themselves for these essential purposes; and may enable every instrument employed in its administration to execute with success, the functions allotted to his charge.*

*In tendering this homage to the Great Author of every public and private good, I assure myself that it expresses your sentiments not less than my own; nor those of my fellow citizens at large, less than either.*

*No people can be bound to acknowledge and adore the Invisible Hand which conducts the affairs of men more than the people of the United States. Every step by which they have advanced to the character of an independent nation seems to have been distinguished by some token of providential agency.*

*And in the important revolution just accomplished, in the system of their United government, the tranquil deliberations and voluntary consent of so many distinct communities, from which the event has resulted, can not be compared with the means by which most governments have been established, without some return of pious*

*gratitude, along with an humble anticipation of
the future blessings which the past seem to
presage ...*

*We ought to be no less persuaded that the
propitious smiles of Heaven can never be
expected on a nation that disregards the eternal
rules of order and right which Heaven itself has
ordained; and since the preservation of the
sacred fire of liberty and the destiny of the
republican model of government are justly
considered as deeply, perhaps finally, staked on
the experiment...*

President George Washington, on October 3, 1789,
from the City of New York, proclaimed a National Day
of Thanksgiving:

*Whereas it is the duty of all nations to
acknowledge the providence of Almighty
God, to obey His will, to be grateful for his
benefits, and humbly to implore His protection
and favor...*

*Now, therefore, I do recommend and assign
Thursday, the twenty-sixth day of November
next, to be devoted by the people of these
Unites States...that we then may all unite unto*

*him our sincere and humble thanks for His kind
care and protection of the people of this
country previous to their becoming a nation;
for the signal and manifold mercies and the
favorable interpositions of His providence in
the course and conclusion of the late war; for
the great degree of tranquility, union, and
plenty which we have since enjoyed; for the
peaceable and rational manner in which we
have been enabled to establish constitutions of
government for our safety and happiness, and
particularly the national one now lately
instituted; for the civil and religious liberty
with which we are blessed...*

*And also that we may then unite in most
humbly offering our prayers and supplications
to the great Lord and Ruler of Nations, and
beseech Him to pardon our national and other
transgressions...to promote the knowledge and
practice of the true religion and virtue...*

*Given under my hand, at the City of New York,
the 3rd of October, A.D. 1789.*

George Washington kept a personal prayer book,
written in his own handwriting, for each day of the
week. Here are some excerpts, which provide insight

into the depth of his Christian faith:

> *SUNDAY MORNING...Almighty God, and most merciful Father, who didst command the children of Israel to offer a daily sacrifice to Thee, that thereby they might glorify and praise Thee for Thy protection both night and day, receive O Lord, my morning sacrifice which I now offer up to Thee;*

> *I yield Thee humble and hearty thanks, that Thou has preserved me from the dangers of the night past and brought me to the light of this day, and the comfort thereof, a day which is consecrated to Thine own service and for Thine own honor.*

> *Let my heart therefore gracious God be so affected with the glory and majesty of it, that I may not do mine own works but wait on Thee, and discharge those weighty duties Thou required of me:*

> *And since Thou art a God of pure eyes, and will be sanctified in all who draw nearer to Thee, who dost not regard the sacrifice of fools, nor hear sinners who tread in Thy courts, pardon I beseech Thee, my sins, remove them*

*from Thy presence, as far as the east is from the
west, and accept of me for the merits of Thy son
Jesus Christ, that when I come into Thy temple
and compass Thine altar, my prayer may come
before Thee as incense, and as I desire Thou
wouldst hear me calling upon Thee in my
prayers, so give me peace to hear the calling
on me in Thy word, that it may be wisdom,
righteousness, reconciliation and peace to the
saving of my soul in the day of the Lord Jesus.*

*Grant that I may hear it with reverence, receive
it with meekness, mingle it with faith, and that
it may accomplish in me gracious God, the
good work for which Thou hast sent it.*

*Bless my family, kindred, friends and country,
be our God and guide this day and forever for
His sake, who lay down in the grave and arose
again for us, Jesus Christ our Lord. Amen.*

*SUNDAY EVENING...O most Glorious God, in
Jesus Christ my merciful and loving Father, I
acknowledge and confess my guilt, in the weak
and imperfect performance of the duties of this
day. I have called on Thee for pardon and
forgiveness of sins....Let me live according to
those holy rules which Thou hast this day*

*prescribed in Thy Holy Word; make me to know what is acceptable in Thy sight, and therein to delight, open the eyes of my understanding, and help me thoroughly to examine myself concerning my knowledge, faith and repentance, increase my faith, and direct me to the true object, Jesus Christ the Way, the Truth and the Life, Bless, O Lord, all the people of this land, from the highest to the lowest, particularly those whom Thou has appointed to rule us in church & state.*

*Continue Thy goodness to me this night. These weak petitions, I humbly implore Thee to hear, accept and answer for the sake of Thy Dear Son, Jesus Christ our Lord, Amen.*

*MONDAY MORNING...O eternal and everlasting God, I presume to present myself this morning before Thy Divine Majesty, beseeching Thee to accept my humble and hearty thanks...direct my thoughts, words and work, wash away my sins in the immaculate Blood of the Lamb, and purge my heart by Thy Holy Spirit...Daily frame me more and more into the likeness of Thy Son, Jesus Christ, that living in Thy fear, and dying in Thy favor, I may in Thy appointed time attain the resurrection of the just unto eternal life. Bless my family, friends and kindred, and unite us all in praising and glorifying Thee in all our works.*

*MONDAY EVENING...Most Gracious Lord God, from whom proceedeth every good and perfect gift, I offer to Thy Divine Majesty my unfeigned praise and thanksgiving for all Thy mercies towards me...I have sinned and done very wickedly, be merciful to me, O God, and pardon me for Jesus Christ's sake...Thou gavest Thy Son to die for me; and hast given me assurance of salvation, upon my repentance and sincerely endeavoring to conform my life to His holy precepts and example...*

*Bless O Lord the whole race of mankind, and let the world be filled with the knowledge of Thee and Thy Son, Jesus Christ...I beseech Thee to defend me this night from all evil, and do more for me than I can think or ask, for Jesus Christ's sake, in whose most Holy Name and Words, I continue to pray, Our Father, who art in heaven, hallowed be Thy Name....*

*TUESDAY MORNING...O Lord our God, most mighty and merciful Father, I, thine unworthy creature and servant, do once more approach*

*Thy presence. Though not worthy to appear
before Thee because of my natural corruptions,
and the many sins and transgressions which I
have committed against Thy Divine Majesty;
yet I beseech Thee, for the sake of Him in whom
Thou are well please, the Lord Jesus Christ, to
admit me to render Thee deserved thanks and
praises for Thy manifold mercies extended
toward me....*

*Bless the people of this land, be a Father to the
fatherless, a Comforter to the comfortless, a
Deliverer to the captives, and a Physician to
the sick. Let Thy blessing be upon our friends,
kindred and families. Be our Guide this day
and forever through Jesus Christ in whose
blessed form of prayer I conclude my weak
petitions — Our Father, who art in heaven,
hallowed be Thy Name...*

*TUESDAY EVENING...Most gracious God and
heavenly Father, we cannot cease, but must cry
unto Thee for mercy, because my sins cry
against me for justice...That I may know my
sins are forgiven by His death and passion.
Embrace me in the arms of Thy mercy;
vouchsafe to receive me unto the bosom of Thy
love, shadow me with Thy wings, that I may*

*safely rest under Thy protection this night; and so into Thy hands I commend myself, both soul and body, in the name of Thy son, Jesus Christ, beseeching Thee, when this life shall end, I may take my everlasting rest with Thee in Thy heavenly kingdom. Bless all in authority over us, be merciful to all those afflicted with Thy cross or calamity, bless all my friends, forgive my enemies and accept my thanksgiving this evening for all the mercies and favors afforded me; hear and graciously answer these my requests, and whatever else Thou see'st needful grant us, for the sake of Jesus Christ in whose blessed Name and Words I continue to pray, Our Father, who art in Heaven, hallowed be Thy Name....*

*WEDNESDAY MORNING...Almighty and eternal Lord God, the great Creator of Heaven and Earth, and the God and Father of our Lord Jesus Christ; look down from Heaven, in pity and compassion upon me Thy servant, who humbly prostrate myself before Thee, sensible of Thy mercy and my own misery...*

*Help all in affliction or adversity — give them patience and a sanctified use of their affliction, and in Thy good time, deliverance from them;*

> *forgive my enemies, take me unto Thy*
> *protection this day, keep me in perfect peace,*
> *which I ask in Thy Name for the sake of Jesus.*
> *Amen.*

George Washington wrote about what he felt made America great:

> *It is impossible to rightly govern the world*
> *without God and the Bible.*

> *It is impossible to account for the creation of*
> *the universe, without the agency of a Supreme*
> *Being. It is impossible to govern the universe*
> *without the aid of a Supreme Being. It is*
> *impossible to reason without arriving at a*
> *Supreme Being.*

> *Religion is as necessary to reason, as reason is*
> *to religion. The one cannot exist without the*
> *other. A reasoning being would lose his reason*
> *in attempting to account for the great*
> *phenomena of nature, had he not a Supreme*
> *Being to refer to.*

# DANIEL WEBSTER

Daniel Webster is considered one of the greatest

orators in American history. He was a famous attorney, a member of the U.S. House of Representatives and then the U.S. Senate. He served as Secretary of State for three Presidents. Webster was also a fervent Christian, as his statements below reveal:

> *If there is anything in my thoughts or style to commend, the credit is due to my parents for instilling in me an early love of the Scriptures. If we abide by the principles taught in the Bible, our country will go on prospering and to prosper; but if we and our posterity neglect its instructions and authority, no man can tell how sudden a catastrophe may overwhelm us and bury all our glory in profound obscurity.*

December 22, 1820, to celebrate of the 200 year anniversary of the Pilgrim landing at Plymouth Rock, Webster declared:

> *Lastly, our ancestors established their system of government on morality and religious sentiment. Moral habits, they believed, cannot safely be trusted on any other foundation than religious principle, nor any government be secure which is not supported by moral habits....Whatever makes men good Christians, makes them good citizens...*

*Finally, let us not forget the religious character of our origin. Our fathers were brought hither by their high veneration for the Christian religion. They journeyed by its light, and labored in its hope. They sought to incorporate its principles with the elements of their society, and to diffuse its influence through all their institutions, civil, political, or literary.*

*Let us cherish these sentiments, and extend this influence still more widely; in full conviction that this is the happiest society which partakes in the highest degree of the mild and peaceful spirit of Christianity.*

Webster, on June 17, 1843, at the Bunker Hill Monument in Charleston, Massachusetts, spoke these stirring words about our forefathers' reverence for the Bible:

*The Bible came with them. And it is not to be doubted, that to free and universal reading of the Bible, in that age, men were much indebted for right views of civil liberty.*

*The Bible is a book of faith, and a book of doctrine, and a book of morals, and a book of religion, of special revelation from God; but it*